GREGORY HINES

GREGORY HINES

❧

Gina De Angelis

CHELSEA HOUSE PUBLISHERS
Philadelphia

Cover photo: Sandra Johnson/Saga/Archive Photos; inset: Photofest

Chelsea House Publishers

Editor in Chief	Stephen Reginald
Production Manager	Pamela Loos
Director of Photography	Judy L. Hasday
Art Director	Sara Davis
Managing Editor	James D. Gallagher
Senior Production Editor	LeeAnne Gelletly

Staff for GREGORY HINES

Associate Art Director	Takashi Takahashi
Prepared by	21st Century Publishing and Communications, New York
Cover Designer	Robert Gerson

The Chelsea House World Wide Website address is
http://www.chelseahouse.com

First Printing

1 3 5 7 9 8 6 4 2

Library of Congress Cataloging-in-Publication Data

De Angelis, Gina.
Gregory Hines / by Gina De Angelis.
p. cm. – (Black Americans of achievement)
Includes bibliographical references and index.
ISBN 0-7910-5197-8 (hc) – ISBN 0-7910-5198-6 (pbk.)
1. Hines, Gregory. 2. Motion picture actors and actresses—United
States—Biography—Juvenile literature. 3. Dancers—United
States—Biography—Juvenile literature. 4.Afro-America motion
picture actors and actresses—United States—Biography—Juvenile
literature. 5. Afro-American dancers—United States—Biography—
Juvenile literature.
I. Title. II. Series.
PN2287.H53D43   1999
791.43'028'092—dc21

[B]

99-17790
CIP
AC

Frontis:
Onstage, the multitalented Gregory Hines explodes into action as dancer, actor, and singer.

CONTENTS

BLACK AMERICANS OF ACHIEVEMENT

HENRY AARON
baseball great

KAREEM ABDUL-JABBAR
basketball great

MUHAMMAD ALI
heavyweight champion

RICHARD ALLEN
*religious leader and
social activist*

MAYA ANGELOU
author

LOUIS ARMSTRONG
musician

ARTHUR ASHE
tennis great

JOSEPHINE BAKER
entertainer

JAMES BALDWIN
author

TYRA BANKS
model

BENJAMIN BANNEKER
scientist and mathematician

AMIRI BARAKA
poet and playwright

COUNT BASIE
bandleader and composer

ROMARE BEARDEN
artist

JAMES BECKWOURTH
frontiersman

MARY MCLEOD BETHUNE
educator

GEORGE WASHINGTON
CARVER
botanist

CHARLES CHESNUTT
author

JOHNNIE COCHRAN
lawyer

BILL COSBY
entertainer

PAUL CUFFE
merchant and abolitionist

MILES DAVIS
musician

FATHER DIVINE
religious leader

FREDERICK DOUGLASS
abolitionist editor

CHARLES DREW
physician

W. E. B. DU BOIS
scholar and activist

PAUL LAURENCE DUNBAR
poet

DUKE ELLINGTON
bandleader and composer

RALPH ELLISON
author

JULIUS ERVING
basketball great

LOUIS FARRAKHAN
political activist

ELLA FITZGERALD
singer

MORGAN FREEMAN
actor

MARCUS GARVEY
black nationalist leader

JOSH GIBSON
baseball great

WHOOPI GOLDBERG
entertainer

CUBA GOODING JR.
actor

ALEX HALEY
author

PRINCE HALL
social reformer

JIMI HENDRIX
musician

MATTHEW HENSON
explorer

GREGORY HINES
performer

BILLIE HOLIDAY
singer

LENA HORNE
entertainer

WHITNEY HOUSTON
singer and actress

LANGSTON HUGHES
poet

ZORA NEALE HURSTON
author

JANET JACKSON
singer

JESSE JACKSON
civil-rights leader and politician

MICHAEL JACKSON
entertainer

SAMUEL L. JACKSON
actor

T. D. JAKES
religious leader

JACK JOHNSON
heavyweight champion

MAGIC JOHNSON
basketball great

SCOTT JOPLIN
composer

BARBARA JORDAN
politician

MICHAEL JORDAN
basketball great

CORETTA SCOTT KING
civil-rights leader

MARTIN LUTHER KING JR.
civil-rights leader

LEWIS LATIMER
scientist

SPIKE LEE
filmmaker

CARL LEWIS
champion athlete

JOE LOUIS
heavyweight champion

RONALD MCNAIR
astronaut

MALCOLM X
militant black leader

BOB MARLEY
musician

THURGOOD MARSHALL
Supreme Court justice

TONI MORRISON
author

ELIJAH MUHAMMAD
religious leader

EDDIE MURPHY
entertainer

JESSE OWENS
champion athlete

SATCHEL PAIGE
baseball great

CHARLIE PARKER
musician

ROSA PARKS
civil-rights leader

COLIN POWELL
military leader

PAUL ROBESON
singer and actor

JACKIE ROBINSON
baseball great

CHRIS ROCK
comedian/actor

DIANA ROSS
entertainer

WILL SMITH
actor

CLARENCE THOMAS
Supreme Court justice

SOJOURNER TRUTH
antislavery activist

HARRIET TUBMAN
antislavery activist

NAT TURNER
slave revolt leader

TINA TURNER
entertainer

DENMARK VESEY
slave revolt leader

ALICE WALKER
author

MADAM C. J. WALKER
entrepreneur

BOOKER T. WASHINGTON
educator

DENZEL WASHINGTON
actor

J. C. WATTS
politician

VANESSA WILLIAMS
singer and actress

OPRAH WINFREY
entertainer

TIGER WOODS
golf star

RICHARD WRIGHT
author

ON
ACHIEVEMENT

————— ❦ —————

Coretta Scott King

BEFORE YOU BEGIN this book, I hope you will ask yourself what the word *excellence* means to you. I think it's a question we should all ask, and keep asking as we grow older and change. Because the truest answer to it should never change. When you think of excellence, perhaps you think of success at work; or of becoming wealthy; or meeting the right person, getting married, and having a good family life.

Those goals are worth striving for, but there is a better way to look at excellence. As Martin Luther King Jr. said in one of his last sermons, "I want you to be first in love. I want you to be first in moral excellence. I want you to be first in generosity. If you want to be important, wonderful. If you want to be great, wonderful. But recognize that he who is greatest among you shall be your servant."

My husband knew that the true meaning of achievement is service. When I met him, in 1952, he was already ordained as a Baptist minister and was working toward a doctoral degree at Boston University. I was studying at the New England Conservatory and dreamed of accomplishments in music. We married a year later, and after I graduated the following year we moved to Montgomery, Alabama. We didn't know it then, but our notions of achievement were about to undergo a dramatic change.

You may have read or heard about what happened next. What began with the boycott of a local bus line grew into a national crusade, and by the time he was assassinated in 1968 my husband had fashioned a black movement powerful enough to shatter forever the practice of racial segregation. What you may not have read about is where he learned to resist injustice without compromising his religious beliefs.

He adopted a strategy of nonviolence from a man of a different race, who lived in a different country and even practiced a different religion. The man was Mahatma Gandhi, the great leader of India, who devoted his life to serving humanity in the spirit of love and nonviolence. It was in these principles that Martin discovered his method for social reform. More than anything else, those two principles were the key to his achievements.

These books are about African Americans who served society through the excellence of their achievements. They form part of the rich history of black men and women in America—a history of stunning accomplishments in every field of human endeavor, from literature and art to science, industry, education, diplomacy, athletics, jurisprudence, even polar exploration.

Not all of the people in this history had the same ideals, but I think you will find that all of them had something in common. Like Martin Luther King Jr., they all decided to become "drum majors" and serve humanity. In that principle—whether it was expressed in books, inventions, or song—they found a goal and a guide outside themselves that showed them a way to serve others instead of living only for themselves.

Reading the stories of these courageous men and women not only helps us discover the principles that we will use to guide our own lives; it also teaches us about our black heritage and about America itself. It is crucial for us to know the heroes and heroines of our history and to realize that the price we paid in our struggle for equality in America was dear. But we must also understand that we have gotten as far as we have partly because America's democratic system and ideals made it possible.

We are still struggling with racism and prejudice. But the great men and women in this series are a tribute to the spirit of the country in which they have flourished. And that makes their stories special and worth knowing.

1

THE PERFORMANCE
OF A LIFETIME

T HE AUDIENCE WAITED expectantly as film star Signourney Weaver opened the envelope. Its contents would reveal the winner of the 1992 Tony Awards for Best Actor in a Musical. "And the Tony goes to Gregory Hines!"

After more than four decades in show business, the lean and lithe tap dancer, actor, and singer had finally earned the coveted award. Hines had been nominated before, for his outstanding performances in the shows *Eubie, Comin' Uptown, and Sophisticated Ladies,* but the honors had gone to others. He remembered how he had felt three times in a row when another person's name had been called: "It was such a harsh sound and the rush of emotion was such that it actually hurt." This time it was his turn, and it was different. "When I heard my own name, I got this warm rush that went through my whole body," he recalled.

It was Hines's mesmerizing performance as Ferdinand "Jelly Roll" Morton in the hit musical *Jelly's Last Jam* that netted him the Tony. Not only was the role a career breakthrough for Hines, the production itself was a breakthrough in African-American musical theater. Until then, black musicals (except for *Dreamgirls*) had been revues—shows that celebrated music rather than people. *Jelly's Last Jam,* honored with 11 Tony nominations, was called by *The New York Times* "The breakthrough musical of our time."

A joyful Gregory Hines accepts the 1992 Tony Award for Best Actor in a Musical for his starring role in Jelly's Last Jam, *a performance that marked a career breakthrough after more than 40 years in show business. With him is Faith Prince, winner for Best Actress in a Musical.*

The show explored the conflicts and inner lives of black Americans by portraying the life, character, and music of Jelly Roll Morton, a jazz pianist, composer, and the self-proclaimed inventor of jazz.

Morton was born Ferdinand Joseph LaMothe in New Orleans in 1890 into a Creole family. Creoles were descendants of African slaves and white French masters. In early New Orleans, Creoles had all the rights and privileges of whites. By the time Morton was born, segregation and racial laws in Louisiana had deprived Creoles of most of their status as whites and placed them in the same category as blacks. Many Creoles, however, clung to their French heritage, turning from the culture and traditions of their black ancestors. Morton was born into this atmosphere of racial and class tensions.

A light-skinned Creole, Morton too denied his blackness. Yet he was drawn to the vibrant music and rhythms of his African-American ancestors. From black musicians he learned blues and ragtime and listened to the music of New Orleans black brass bands. He absorbed the sounds of the "rag man," the "gator man," the "gumbo lady" as they cried their wares in the city streets. He frequented the notorious district of saloons and brothels called Storyville, mingling with gamblers, dealers, pool sharks, prostitutes, and hustlers. When Morton was about 15, his great-grandmother threw him out of her house because he associated with what his family called the "lower orders" and people of darker skin. He then began his musical journey as pianist, composer, arranger, band leader, and recording artist.

Morton, who took the name "Jelly Roll" because "Jelly" was black slang for sex, was a controversial figure. Boasting of his French ancestry, he consistently denied his African-American roots and exaggerated his Creole background. He once told an interviewer, "All my folks came directly from the shores of France."

He also claimed that the original spelling of his name was "La Menthe" because it sounded more French than "LaMothe." Yet he sought the company of disreputable people and began his career in Storyville. And he drew much of his music from African-American roots. But his greatest boast was that he had invented jazz, and all his life he made this claim. Although jazz was born in New Orleans, many musicians and composers were involved in its birth, and jazz historians do not agree that Morton invented jazz. However, he brilliantly combined the blues and ragtime and New Orleans sounds with the more formal music of his French heritage to create an innovative form of jazz. He is considered the most important of the New Orleans jazz composers and

Portraying jazz legend Jelly Roll Morton, Hines shares an exuberant dance number with 18-year-old Savion Glover (left), who played the young Jelly Roll in the highly acclaimed Broadway musical.

Jazz pioneer Ferdinand "Jelly Roll" Morton recorded many of his songs in the 1920s and 1930s. In addition to his talents as a pianist, band leader, and arranger, he was a prolific composer whose songs include the well-known "Jelly Roll Blues."

arrangers and, as Morton himself put it, "The world's greatest hot tune writer."

To produce a play about this contradictory and not always sympathetic figure was a challenge to the producers of *Jelly's Last Jam* and to its star, Gregory Hines. When he first read the script, Hines rejected the role because he did not like the character. He finally relented when his wife Pamela Koslow, who was also co-producer of the play, persuaded him to attend a workshop performance and meet with writer-director George Wolfe. Hines was impressed with Wolfe's talent. He also knew Wolfe was taking a risk in presenting a new kind of black musical. *Jelly* was not to be the stereotypical black musical. As Hines said, "For too long on the musical stage we have perpetuated the myth that African Americans are always singing and dancing and happy." Rather, through the contradictory character of Morton, the play explores an extremely sensitive issue in black America—internal racial conflict. Hines later reflected on the play and his role in it.

> I loved being in shows like *Eubie* and *Sophisticated Ladies*, but I knew they weren't really saying anything. *Jelly* is. One of the best kept secrets in the world is the racism that exists within the African-American community. And I knew that to have a piece on Broadway about the attitudes we have about hair quality and skin color and class would not only affect white and African-American audiences, but it would speak on larger issues of the human condition.

Hines also remembers that in his own family light skin versus dark skin was an issue, and he explained: "My mother came from a very light-skinned background. My father is dark-skinned, and when they fell in love her father refused to come to the wedding." For Hines, performing in the musical was not just an opportunity to use his talents as an actor and dancer in a major production. It gave him the chance to speak to the issue of racial conflicts within the African-American community.

Jelly's Last Jam is the journey through Morton's life. As the play opens, Morton is near death when a sinister figure called the Chimney Man appears and beckons him with the words, "Welcome, Jelly, to the other side. Time to tell your tale 'n' save your soul." As the play moves back through Jelly's life, the Chimney Man hovers nearby, constantly reminding Jelly of how he has denied his blackness.

Despite his commitment to the role, Hines did have difficult moments. He thought about his own family as he had to express Morton's racial attitudes.

During rehearsals, Hines had trouble with such lines as "I [Morton] was classically trained while those of a darker hue lived in shacks and crooned the blues." Still, Hines overcame his anxieties, and sometimes even anger, as he delved into the role. He explained, "After I really got inside Jelly, I enjoyed saying his lines."

Some who followed Morton's life and career did not agree with the concept of the play and the way Jelly's character was portrayed. Bob Greene, an expert on Morton's life and music, created and toured with his own show, *The World of Jelly Roll Morton*. Greene criticized the play. "Jelly was not racist," he insisted. "He was a New Orleans Creole and all his recordings were with Black musicians. His idol was the pianist Tony Jackson, fully Black. . . . In contradiction to the very premise of the play, he knew his roots and drew his music from them." Hines and director Wolfe disagreed. "I think the play follows the truth very closely," Hines explained. "In fact, I think there have been areas of Jelly's actual life that have been softened to make him as palatable as he can be and yet still tell the story of his life."

Whatever the realities of Jelly's life, Hines faced difficulties other than the script. He had to do eight shows a week, and he was not in top physical condition. To prepare, he redesigned his diet and began lifting weights to get in shape. Another challenge facing Hines and director Wolfe was the fact that Morton was a pianist, not a tap dancer. Hines had to portray Morton's character through tap dancing, as well as acting and singing, rather than through playing the piano. Wolfe decided that none of the tap dances would be just for fun. Each was to express emotions and concepts. It worked. For two hours and 25 minutes every night, Hines tapped across the stage in his own distinctive style, shoulders a little

still, legs moving in graceful motions. Critic John Simon of *New York* magazine called Hines "the consummate leading man. Acting, dancing, singing, or just standing in emotion-filled stillness, he puts into this Jelly Roll a part of himself that is deeper than the part."

Playing Jelly Roll Morton was perhaps the crowning moment of a long career full of impressive achievements. How did Hines manage to be in show business for most of his life? Where and why did he learn to tap? And how did he succeed in becoming not just the premier tap dancer of his generation but a successful movie actor and a solid role model for young African Americans?

Television viewers had the opportunity to see Hines's style when he tapped and sang on a PBS special, Jammin': Jelly Roll Morton on Broadway. *Here, Hines (in the striped suit) leads the cast in a rousing ensemble number.*

2

THE EARLIEST YEARS: WHY TAP?

GREGORY OLIVER HINES was born on Valentine's Day in 1946 in New York City, the second son of Alma Iola and Maurice Hines. The family lived in Washington Heights, a fairly integrated neighborhood on Manhattan's Upper West Side. The neighborhood is near Harlem, which was the home of some of the most famous African-American entertainers, including singer Ethel Waters and jazz great Louis Armstrong. Several well-known tap dancers also lived there, among them the Nicholas Brothers, famous for combining traditional tap dancing with ballet and energetic acrobatics, and Bill "Bojangles" Robinson, known for his seemingly effortless tapping.

Alma and Maurice Hines decided it would be a good idea for Gregory's older brother, Maurice Jr., to learn tap dancing, and they signed him up for lessons. He was just over four years old. Hines's mother recalls the first day Maurice Jr. went for tap lessons. Gregory was two and a half—too young to take lessons—but he cried until the teacher let him in. Alma said, "I looked in the door, and Greg was holding on to his brother's hand doing the tap, and with his other hand he had his thumb in his mouth." Little Gregory was still too young to actually take lessons, but he copied a lot of tap steps from his brother.

Apparently the boys had an inborn talent for the art as well as an aptitude for learning. Their paternal

Gregory Hines checks out a young contestant at a tap-dance contest. His own childhood experiences as a professional tap dancer have given him a special feeling for youngsters who want to learn to tap dance and who, as Hines hopes, will continue to keep the art form alive and well.

19

grandmother, Ora Hines, had been a showgirl at Harlem's famed Cotton Club during the 1920s. And their father, although working as a grocery clerk when Gregory was born, had musical ambitions. There was another consideration, as Gregory later recalled, "There was the feeling maybe this could be a way of earning a living."

The elder Hines, who had changed jobs to become a bouncer at the Audubon Theatre and Ballroom in Harlem, sometimes got the boys onto the stage during fashion shows. Their performances were short, but they did earn a little money. The brothers' careers in show business had begun. After lessons with Henry LeTang, considered by many to be the greatest tap-dancing teacher in the world, the Hines boys began performing professionally. Maurice Jr. was eight, Gregory was six.

Billing themselves as the Hines Kids, they began appearing at Harlem's famed Apollo Theater. The theater served as a kind of day-care center for the boys. Their mother took them there after school and then picked them up after their last show. At the Apollo, the boys had the chance to watch many famous performers, including Sammy Davis Jr., whom Gregory wanted to emulate.

In 1955, at Alma's suggestion, the boys began making the rounds of the nightclubs, performing only on weekends during the school year and touring more extensively during summer vacations. Around this time, Gregory had an accident that would affect his vision for the rest of his life. While playing one day, he fell on a tree stump, which penetrated his right eye. His busy dancing schedule was not interrupted, however. The accident happened during the school year, when the boys were working only on weekends.

Besides performing in nightclubs, Maurice Jr. and Gregory appeared on television's *Jackie Gleason*

Show and even did some stints in Europe. As the boys grew older, they changed the name of their act. When "we started to get pimples," Gregory later commented, they began calling themselves the Hines Brothers.

The years on the road must have been hard on the family. Alma traveled with the boys and Maurice Sr. stayed at home. The separations did have a bright side, however. While he was on his own, Maurice Sr. learned to play the drums. This way he could join the

Tap-dance legends such as Bill "Bojangles" Robinson and the dance duo of Buck and Bubbles appeared regularly at Harlem's Apollo Theater as did singers Bessie Smith, Billie Holiday, and Ethel Waters. And Wednesday amateur nights launched the careers of Ella Fitzgerald, Sarah Vaughan, and James Brown.

act so that the family could stay together while touring. In 1963, when Gregory's father came on board, the act was renamed Hines, Hines and Dad—with Maurice Jr. playing the "straight man" to Gregory's "comic relief." The trio toured for several years, playing Las Vegas and appearing on *The Tonight Show* with Johnny Carson. Gregory insists, however, that "We weren't ever *really* successful. . . . We were a very strong opening act, but we never got over the hump."

How does Gregory Hines feel about working as a professional during his childhood? Does he think his parents pushed him too hard? Not too hard, Hines said in 1985. His parents signed their sons up for lessons "like parents give kids violin lessons, and when we showed a little aptitude they just decided to see if it was something we could use. . . . Our mother wanted us to have an outlet," said Gregory. His brother Maurice added, "to get us out of the ghetto." Gregory explains that their mother was particularly supportive of her sons' talents but did not push them into the business unwillingly. Does he feel, like many young performers do later on, that he missed out on having a carefree childhood? Not really. "It was fun," he said in a 1996 interview. "It didn't feel like a job, even though we were on the road appearing in nightclubs all over the country. We had a childhood too, so it was great," he later told another interviewer:

> My mother was able to make it enjoyable. My brother and I would come offstage at the Apollo—we were doing four shows a day. She would take off our clothes, rub us down with alcohol, put our bathrobes on and comic books in our hands, and feed us from the two-eye burner she had in the dressing room.

Hines spent most of his childhood in Washington Heights. He often claims, however, that he grew up in Harlem. "I don't know where he gets this Harlem bit," said his mother in 1986. Certainly he spent a

great deal of time and energy at the Apollo Theater, where he learned so much from his mentors and other performers. Perhaps he feels, as an African American, that he can more strongly identify with the neighborhood of Harlem than with the one he lived in. In fact, Hines does have white ancestry on his mother's side. Her ancestors were Jewish, Panamanian, Irish, and Portuguese—not solely African American. Hines explains his feelings about his own racial identity: "I have always considered myself a black man. What my mother has on her side is irrelevant. When I go for a role that was written for a white, it means nothing."

The young Hines brothers attended Willard Mace, a special school for professional children. At the time, they were the only blacks. Later, the boys attended the Quintano School for Young Professionals,

From left, Maurice Sr., Maurice Jr., and Gregory—Hines, Hines and Dad. They were well known as a touring trio, but together they never really made it to the top in show business.

Young Gregory experienced racial prejudice on a tour in Florida when he was forced to use the "Colored Only" water fountain. It was his first real brush with segregation and discrimination.

where other future performers such as Patty Duke and Bernadette Peters also studied. Hines claims he felt at ease around white people and was accepted because of his talent and charm.

Nevertheless, racism was still a prevalent attitude. From traveling and performing, the Hines boys learned about the world of entertainment and of tap dancing in particular. There was another world, however, and Gregory and Maurice Jr. were soon exposed to it. As Hines later put it in simple terms, "Miami. Nineteen-fifty-seven. That's where I *really* discovered what was happening."

Segregation was still the law of the land, particularly in the Deep South. African Americans were forced to live apart from whites; they could not travel in white areas without police passes. In 1957, 11-year-old Gregory and the cast of his revue were picking up their passes in a police station in Miami Beach. Being thirsty, young Gregory headed for a water fountain—the white one. Since the fountain for blacks was labeled "Colored," Gregory thought the water might be some sort of color. "I got within a few feet, and about twenty of the black people in the show came running over and grabbed me," he recalls. "And I figured *the whole thing out*."

Later Hines remarked of the incident that "Those were the conditions. You lived within those conditions and pushed to change, but you knew the score."

On the whole, Hines feels that "it was a wonderful childhood." He spent most of his time learning more about the history of tap dancing as well as the techniques, and he realizes that he had the rare opportunity to meet and interact with his idols. "I grew up surrounded by great black tap dancers," Hines said in a 1986 interview. His tap teacher, the legendary Henry LeTang, told him and his brother that "You two better learn to really dance, because now you're cute, but cute's not for long."

Gregory Hines took his teacher's words to heart, becoming one of the foremost if not *the* foremost interpreter of modern tap. In the 1990s, there has been a resurgence of popularity in tap dancing. Much of it can be attributed to the work of Gregory Hines.

3

DEVELOPING A STYLE

GREGORY HINES HAS his own ideas about the evolution of tap dancing. When asked if tap is a black tradition, he responded:

> I don't know. There's always been an argument as to who invented tap dancing. I went out to dinner with Gene Kelly once . . . he felt that it had come from the Irish clog dances. I have always felt that African-American tap dancers took tap dancing and tried to express themselves in a spontaneous and improvisational way. And because our experience is so intertwined with jazz music, which is an American art form, there was a fusion between tap dancers and jazz musicians that kicked tap dancing to another level in terms of growth. So, as an African-American tap dancer, I'm very proud of our contribution.

If Gene Kelly believed that tap dancing has its roots in Irish dancing, and Hines believes that African Americans created jazz tap, both are likely correct. Like any American art form, it appears that tap was created by many people of different ethnic origins. One tap historian, Rusty Frank, has analyzed tap as the meshing of many different dance styles brought to the United States by people of predominantly African, English, Irish, and Scottish origin. Later, these styles mingled with ragtime, jazz, swing, and bebop to evolve into modern tap. Frank also believes that tap took its spirit from the rhythms

Looming over nighttime 42nd Street, a billboard image of Hines breaks into the dance style that took him years to develop. Blending improvisation with sophisticated and calculated moves, Hines calls his style "improvography."

and tempo of the Machine Age in the United States, what he calls the "clickety-clack of electric streetcars, the crash and pound of the subway, the riveting cry of buildings going up and coming down."

Tap's origins in the 1800s show that improvisation and competition were a key to its development. Jane Goldberg, a tap historian, writes that tap "came out of the lower classes, developed in competitive 'battles' on street corners by Irish immigrants and African-American slaves." From tap's earliest roots in the 1800s, "challenges" and "stealing steps" were common. One-upmanship was a hallmark of tap, and stealing steps did not mean just imitating others. A dancer always added his or her own spin to the steps. As early as the 1840s, tap originator William Henry "Juba" Lane and Irish step dancer Jack Diamond challenged each other in dance competitions in Boston and New York City. Neither was a clear winner.

African Americans and Irish immigrants had a great deal in common in the 19th century. As slaves, African Americans were forbidden to play drums, an integral part of most African music and dance. Instead they developed a form of dance involving hand clapping and foot tapping. In Ireland, the British rulers of the island outlawed Irish cultural activities such as playing traditional Irish music and dancing. In the United States too, both groups were mostly poor, and the majority of white society looked upon them as outcasts. Over time, Irish clog dancing and African-American dance and syncopation melded together. With additions along the way by a variety of artists, the art form we know today as tap evolved.

Whatever its deepest roots, tap is a distinctly modern form of dance. Tap reached its peak popularity—so far—in the first decades of the 20th century. Particularly after World War I, during the "Roaring Twenties," jazz became more and more popular, and jazz dance—what we know as tap dancing—took the youth culture by storm. This style of dance had spread from the minstrel shows of the late 19th century to the vaudeville shows of the early 20th to the concert stage and later to Broadway musicals. These were the earliest years of Hollywood films as well. The film industry was expanding across the nation—and spreading to other countries. Hollywood reflected what Americans wanted to see: tap dancing. Films also helped spread tap's popularity as people wanted to see live what they saw in films. Wherever audiences wanted entertainment, tap artists—"hoofers"—were there, dancing their way through small towns and large cities.

Although the "golden age" of tap dancing in Hollywood musicals was probably the 1930s and 1940s, the Hines family was able to make a living touring and tapping into the 1970s. Gregory and Maurice Jr. were born at a time when tap was a hot form of entertainment and therefore a viable profession. Although it is a form of expression that is still evolving today, tap was perhaps even more fluid and formative in those years.

Who were some of those dancers who helped develop tap into what it is today? Who were Hines's mentors? Who influenced him the most?

> I met Sammy Davis Jr. when I was about nine years old, and it seemed that every time I was in his company, I learned from him. He was extremely generous with his knowledge and experiences. I idolized him. . . . He knew that I idolized him, but he was never in any way aloof with me; he was never intimidating. I always felt that he was a real person, and in many ways, that's shaped me. Because in this business, where someone is in front of the public a lot and blown up and praised, some people begin to feel distanced. They begin to think that that person is not human. Sammy Davis was so sincere and honest with me, it touched me in a way that shaped me as a person and as an artist.

In an affectionate moment, Hines gets a hug from Sammy Davis Jr. (left), one of Gregory's idols since childhood. Like Hines, Davis too was a child tapper who appeared in a family act.

Other dancers Hines includes among his heroes are Harold and Fayard Nicholas, Jimmy Slyde, and Bunny Briggs. Each of these artists contributed an individual style to tap. The Nicholas Brothers were known as "The Show Stoppers" at the legendary Cotton Club in Harlem and made several films during the 1930s and 1940s. One of these, *Stormy Weather*, made in 1943, features a fantastic dance sequence in which the brothers' fast-paced dancing is punctuated with incredible leaps and splits. Jimmy Slyde also incorporated elaborate slides in his dancing; these soon became his trademark. Bunny Briggs, too, was unique in his elegant, gentle style of tapping that accompanied many of the most famous "big bands."

One might wonder if being surrounded by older, more experienced dancers and entertainers was intimidating for the younger Hines brother. How did the boys manage to get along with each other and still develop their own individual styles? Gregory has explained the differences: "Oh, yeah. My style of tap is more improvisational. . . . My brother had much more of a choreographic aspect, working things out beforehand . . ." He also explained that a hallmark of great tap dancing is individuality, recalling: "Well, one of the things about tap dancers, they just have so many different styles. Bill Robinson was up on his toes. John Bubbles, of Buck and Bubbles . . . was down on his heels. So you learned very early on to respect everybody's style."

Both were greatly influenced by the stars of the fifties, whom they saw and interacted with at the Apollo Theater. The young Gregory marveled at the discipline of the performers he saw there. As he recalled later:

> One day, at the first show, I see this guy Teddy Hale, and I think, "Wow, he's tremendous!" Comes out for the second show—and does a completely different dance! I can't figure it out! By the third show, I figure out that he doesn't *have* an act—he just makes it up as he goes along. I had no barometer to measure this guy. And from that point on, I decided that I wanted to *be* Teddy Hale.

And when Hines was performing over school vacations, his backstage time was well spent. He made it a point to approach dancers and ask them to draw him some steps. Then he went off by himself and made up routines.

Hines also had the more usual experience of watching his heroes on television. "I've stolen lots of steps from greats like Fred Astaire, Gene Kelly, and the Nicholas Brothers. I watched them on TV and learned from them," he admitted to an interviewer.

So what *is* Gregory Hines's signature style? What makes his dancing unmistakably his? He is known for dancing what he terms "improvography"—he coined the word himself. He prefers to do "riffs," like a jazz musician does with a well-known melody. He takes liberties with rhythms, making up his steps as he goes. Such improvisation is considered the highest form of creation, demanding that a tapper's imagination become instant choreography. One writer has written that "It is the most difficult aspect of tap to master."

Hines is well known for experimenting with rhythm. In fact, he is one of the first tap dancers to radically alter the "rules" of tap dancing. He recalls the first time he did it: "The first time I experimented with what I like to think of as 'No Time' was on the *Tonight Show.* I just decided to let it go. I was dancing in tempo, then I would stop in the step and go with a new tempo." Other dancers were upset at what seemed like a lapse; they even asked him if he had been drunk. "I took that as encouragement in a way," he recalls, "because up until that time, everybody was just saying, 'Boy, were you great! I just love that tap dancing!'" As far as Hines was concerned, he had presented a challenge, and that was what interested him.

Hines's style is enormously popular with audiences. He can be tough at one moment, slapping his feet hard on the floor, or smooth and sexy as he delicately glides over the stage. The tones and rhythms of his tapping shift as he moves his lean, flexible body in imaginative flights across the floor,

often breaking out of the classic 4/4 tempo of jazz. When Hines croons as he dances, audiences become intent on catching every word of his lyrics.

In the same unconventional style, Hines refuses to use smiling as a performance tool. He seems to have felt this way at a young age. He says that when he was a teenager, his family insisted he smile while performing, and he didn't want to. "The image always

The Nicholas Brothers often appeared with the big bands. In addition to their leaps and splits, they exhibited their grace and agility by dancing on tabletops.

presented of the tap dancer is as happy, as smiling. It's always phony," he said. Consequently, Hines prefers to let the mood of the dance dictate whether he smiles or not. He has explained that in his dancing, some steps might "give joy, connect me up with something," or there might be " a darkness to them. I hear a minor chord and I dance it." Sometimes Hines grins or shouts with pleasure but generally he dances with his head down, focusing on the sounds of his tapping feet.

Almost everything about Hines's dancing is unconventional in terms of the history and rules of tap. Looking at the style of Fred Astaire and Ginger Rogers, or perhaps Gene Kelly, a viewer will immediately notice a big difference between the Hollywood style of tap dancing in the 1930s and 1940s and the newer, jazz-tap, improvisational style typified by artists like Gregory Hines. The delicate, well-dressed tapping of these older tap stars gave way in the 1970s to a newer, more urban style. Hines, for example, dances in tight sleeveless T-shirts and pleated, baggy trousers.

A journalist has described Gregory's well-known percussive style and how it differs from the stereotypical, smiling tap dancer in a tuxedo and top hat: "He taps hunkered over, bent at the waist, head cocked to the side, arms held loose, almost dangling. Although his feet play a range of sounds from delicate scrapes to fortissimo slaps, he seems to love it best when he is thwacking down the metal." Hines has said that when he is hitting the floor, he wishes he "could bend far enough to get my ear right next to the floor and hear it stomp!" Hines's willingness, and his ability, to push the outer limits of what people expect from tap dancing have made him one of the most popular tap dancers of the late 1900s.

During the 1960s, rock and roll became more and more popular and tap dancing began to fade in comparison. The Hines, Hines and Dad act began to add more comedy and jazz to its routines, reflecting what audiences wanted to see. Along with tap's declining

With his signature tux and top hat, the elegant Fred Astaire was the dean of tappers in the musical films of the 1930s and 1940s as well as on Broadway and later on television. Although he watched and learned from Astaire's movements, Hines radically changed the Astaire style of tap dancing.

Unrestricted by bulky outfits, Hines's dancing reflects his idea that a dancer's body should be seen. His own body is muscular and lean, and he uses it dramatically to experiment with style.

popularity, fewer people were learning to tap dance during the 1950s and 1960s: there was something of a "tap drought."

Young Gregory Hines was a little distracted too. He was discovering young women. During a stint at a resort in the Catskills in the late 1960s, Gregory's mother was there every weekend to do her son's laundry. One day, however, Hines was lured into the laundry room by a bunch of guys who told him a group of young women was in the room. As Hines described it later: "It was a great meeting place! The girls were showing me how to fold. It was the first independent thing I'd done from my mother, and it felt good."

One of those girls he met in the Catskills, a dance therapist named Patricia Panella, became Mrs. Gregory Hines in 1968. They made their home in New York City and, in 1971, had a daughter, Daria. Within a couple of years, however, the now 27-year-old "comic relief" member of the Hines trio realized that he no longer wanted to work with his brother and father. He later confided: "I knew I didn't want to work with the family, which was traumatic." The course his early life had followed was about to be irrevocably altered.

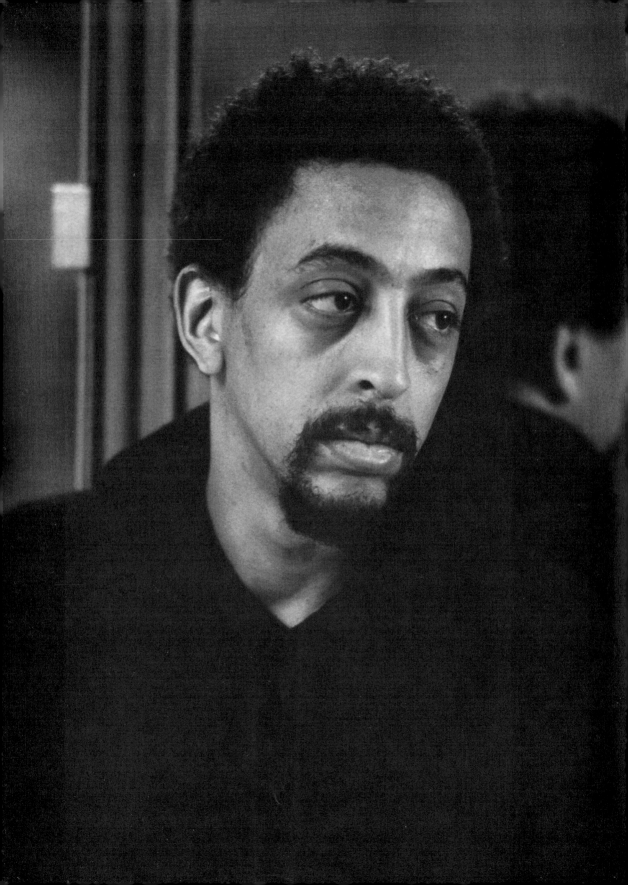

4

AN ENDING AND
A NEW BEGINNING

❦

By 1972 IT seemed that Gregory Hines had everything before him. He was enjoying a promising and successful career, a close family, a wife, and a young daughter—even a dog. And he was, as he said later, desperately unhappy. For some 25 years he had tapped his way across the United States and Europe as part of a routine act with his brother and father that left him feeling locked up. In the early days there was little money; sometimes they had only $600 to split among them. For Gregory, the tedious travel from one unfulfilling job to another was beginning to overwhelm him. He began expressing his discontent by using cocaine to try to escape. Later he commented that "it took about a year for my nose and sinuses to come back."

He and his brother were also at odds with each other and growing apart. Gregory wanted to try his hand at songwriting and become a rock musician. Maurice's ambition was to pursue acting and the legitimate theater. It got so bad that one time, while on tour in San Francisco, Gregory avoided talking to Maurice by crossing the street when he saw him. Shortly thereafter, when they had a fight that nearly ended in blows, Gregory knew the partnership was over.

He was ready to break free from the family act. His marriage too was falling apart. Later he recalled the painful memory of deciding to break away. He

In a quiet moment, Hines's face reflects a pensive mood. Knowing that one career was ending and another was beginning, he had to wonder where the split-up with his family would take him.

was sitting in his kitchen thinking about what to do when Gladys Knight's song "Neither One of Us Wants to Be the First to Say Goodbye" blared from the radio. When he heard the line "Farewell, my love," he broke down in tears. "She was talking about my life. She was just talking to *me*."

So, wrenching though it was, Gregory told his family that he was through with the act. In 1973, with no job, no money, and no real plan, Hines moved to Venice, California. There he founded a jazz-rock band called Severance—with the help, it was reported, of a $5,000 loan from entertainer Bill Cosby. "On a really great week in Venice in five years, I made $40," says Gregory.

During his time in Venice, Hines became a black belt in karate and could have made a decent living teaching the art. Instead, he eked out a living by playing and singing in bars around Los Angeles, writing songs, and sometimes working as a busboy. Although Hines has often said that he does not remember a time when he was not dancing, he also admits that during this period, he "didn't even own a pair of dance shoes."

> I didn't choose to be in the business. I don't remember not dancing. I could always do it. When I got to be about twenty-five, I became very disenchanted. . . . I got interested in the music of the time. I started smokin' dope, I started drinking, I started slowing down and trying to find myself. I didn't want to work in nightclubs. I didn't want to do *Fiddler on the Roof* medleys. I didn't know what I wanted to do. I just knew I was miserable.

Hines was also lonely. He admitted that he "was just so scared of being alone" that he would say anything to a woman companion to keep from having to go home and be by himself. At the same time he took advantage of the hippie lifestyle in its free-and-easy drug use. "Venice Beach was a real charged

atmosphere then. It was music, women, and drugs, and I had my share of all three," Hines says. Once, when his mother called him from New York, he told her, "Look, I just dropped some acid so I can't talk now. " He also indulged in less dangerous excitements, such as having his ear pierced a few times.

It was in Venice that Hines met the woman who would help him overcome that loneliness and eventually become his second wife, Pamela Koslow. Pamela was from a respectable middle-class Jewish family and had grown up on New York City's Upper East Side. She had attended the prestigious Bronx High School of Science, gone on to City College, and then to the University of California at Los Angeles

Despite a party-guy exterior, Hines felt frightened and insecure when he arrived in Venice, California. He could not resist joining hippies like these, who poured into California, and with them he indulged in a do-what-you-want lifestyle.

Hines and Pamela Koslow shared the ups and downs of their hippie lifestyle in Venice. Meeting Pamela was a turning point in Hines's life as he felt he had found the woman he was truly looking for.

for a second degree. She became a student counselor and married an economics professor, who seemed the proper choice for a woman of her background. Later, Pamela could readily understand Gregory's feelings. She too found herself boxed in and stifled. The atmosphere in Los Angeles was far from the propriety of her upbringing, and her marriage and husband seemed too ordinary for her now.

Neither she nor Gregory had any real goals when they met. Pamela was recently divorced and struggling to raise her daughter, Jessica. She was, however, determined not to continue her job counseling students. She had no faith in the very goals she would have to tell students to set. Her philosophy became "Do what you want to do," and she told Gregory, "If you feel like doing nothing, then that's just what you should do." Hines responded instantly. "Here, for the first time," he said later, "was someone who was letting me be me. There were no pressures."

Doing nothing, "being me," and living without pressures, however, did not bring in money. At first, Pamela was able to support Gregory. He recalled that "she would pay my rent, take me out to dinner and buy shoes for Daria." Then he added with a laugh, "She used to tell me she felt she was a patron of the arts." As the money began running out, Pamela had to peddle pottery, clothing, and water pipes along the beach in Venice. Gregory wrote songs that nobody wanted.

When the divorce from Patricia was finalized, Gregory had visitation rights with his daughter Daria. But with his California lifestyle, he could not give her the kind of home he wanted her to have. The first time Daria came to visit from New York, Hines had no place for them to stay. They ended up moving from house to house on the beach. Embarrassed by his circumstances, and afraid that Daria would not be allowed further visits, he asked her not to tell her mother. The little girl responded, "Whenever we crash, can you make sure the people have a TV?" Father and daughter kept their promises to each other.

Aware of his daughter's need for him and of his own needs, Hines joined a group for single fathers. "I had to join them," he said later, "because I love my daughter and I didn't want to make too many mistakes in raising her. Besides, I didn't want to inadvertently put all my attitudes, my hangups, on her." It was a challenge, but as Hines said, "It was fabulous. I felt like I was really learning how to be a father. I discovered the joy of single parenting."

At the same time, Hines also joined a group of

Hines and his grown-up daughter, Daria, enjoy their times together. It was mostly because of Daria, whom he did not want to lose, that Hines gave up his life in California and returned to New York.

men who met to discuss how men treat women. He did it, he explained, to free himself of the burden men often feel about relationships with women and the fear they feel about expressing their feelings. Thanks to his involvement in these groups and the love and support of Pamela, Gregory was beginning to free himself from his fears and insecurities.

There is no question in Hines's mind that the Venice period strengthened him. He explained how:

> I think everybody at some point—especially if they've been working their whole lives—should take time out and think about what they've done. That period of reflection meant a lot to me. I grew up a lot. With the family, I always had a buffer. After a while, I didn't know how to take care of myself. I was twenty-seven years old and very immature. During that period in Venice, I found out how to take care of myself.

The time in Venice may have helped Gregory grow up, but he knew he could not spend his life there. He did not really have a career. His band was performing in clubs and even released an album, which failed. In 1977 the band broke up, and Hines got a job giving guitar lessons. He was rejected for a job as a songwriter for Warner Bros. One day, he and Pamela discovered they had $10 between them. Most importantly, he missed his daughter, and he wanted to move back to New York to be closer to her.

As for making a living in New York, he thought he might give guitar lessons or teach karate. Maurice Hines Jr. had other ideas, however. At the time, Maurice was set for a spot in the road show of the musical *Pippin*. He told Gregory there was plenty of work in New York for tap dancers, and he offered his apartment there to Gregory.

To Gregory's surprise, when he and Pamela arrived in New York Maurice was not on the road after all. He had quit the show after a disagreement with the director. Fortunately for Gregory, Maurice had persuaded his agent to submit Gregory's name to audition for a play called *The Last Minstrel Show*. Gregory described what happened:

> When I auditioned for [*The Last Minstrel Show*], the agent said, "Yeah, you got it, and they've offered $650 a week, but that's not good enough. I'm going to try to get $750 and get your name in a box." I said, "Are you kidding? I don't care about $750, I don't care about a box. I just want this job. Man, if you blow this for me, I'm going to tear your office apart." But he did get $750 and my name in a box.

Gregory was in his element again, tapping and playing drums. Of his comeback, he says: "I hadn't had my tap shoes on for eight years . . . from the time I started back tapping, because of the experience in Venice, I was a different person. It was the first time I felt I had something I wanted to *say*." When *The Last Minstrel Show* closed, Gregory and Maurice appeared next in *Eubie*. Choreographed by his teacher and mentor, Henry LeTang, *Eubie* was a revue based on the songs of pianist and composer Eubie Blake.

For Gregory, getting the role was not all that easy. After his audition, he was sure he had gotten the job. To his surprise, he was turned down. "There must be some mistake," he told the producer, "I was great at the audition. You've got to give me another audition." After many phone calls, the producer agreed. On the second day of rehearsal, Hines was informed that he had the role. His persistence had paid off. To add to Hines's self-confidence, and to his credits, he won a Tony nomination for Best Featured Actor in a Musical for his performance in *Eubie*.

From then on, Gregory Hines's career was in full swing. He emphasized in a later interview that he did not return to New York to get back into show business. Rather, he got back into performing because he found himself in New York with only $40

and no prospects! "To this day I think if I had had three days to consider it [whether to audition], I might have said 'I'd rather not.'"

Whatever the reason for taking up his career again, Hines had learned something from getting the part in *Eubie*: persistence pays off. From then on he would be, as he put it, persistent just short of being obnoxious. His time away from show business had also helped. It pushed him toward what he really wanted to do, and his determination to do what he wanted made him aggressive enough to succeed— twice!—in the tough world of New York show business. Hines's Broadway career soon brought him rave reviews and the attention of entertainment professionals who knew a gem when they found one.

With fellow performers, Hines (center) shows his style in a musical moment from Eubie, *the first musical hit of the 1978–79 Broadway season. The show was Hines's first big career break and brought him his first Tony nomination.*

5

HUMAN LIGHTNING

Hines was propelled into the spotlight in Sophisticated Ladies, *a revue based on the music of Duke Ellington. His jumps and turns and lightning-fast tapping won him excellent reviews and his third Tony nomination. Here he is dancing in the finale with his brother, Maurice Jr. (left).*

HINES'S FIRST FEW years back in New York were filled with his new-found Broadway career. At first, it was difficult tapping again because he had lost some of his physical fitness and resiliency. He adjusted to the rigorous physical work, however, and he knew he had finally found what he wanted to do.

Reviewers fell in love with Hines. Although *The Last Minstrel Show* was a box-office disappointment, Hines himself was praised for his performance. During the successful run of *Eubie*, which opened on Broadway in May 1978, both Gregory and Maurice Jr. earned rave reviews. Influential critic Brendan Gill of *New Yorker* magazine singled out the duo in his review of the show. "The Hines brothers are especially to be praised for their whirling-dervish-like dancing."

Hines's next show, the musical *Comin' Uptown*, opened in November 1979. It was an all-black version of Dickens's *A Christmas Carol* in which Hines played Scrooge. The play was not particularly well received. In fact, it was a monumental flop. One critic, who panned the show for its writing and songs, did praise Hines's performance, however. Commenting that the only reason to see the play was Gregory Hines, he went on to write: "He is a marvelous performer, with an inhumanly agile body and a joi de vivre that appears to be more than mere

Hines joins the Boston Pops Orchestra, dancing and belting out Eubie Blake songs. The program, produced for the PBS television series Evening at the Pops, *was yet another showcase for Hines's talents as a dancer and singer.*

professional [makeup]." Another reviewer urged audiences to see Hines in the role as he praised the dancer's agility and wit and his seeming defiance of the laws of gravity as his tapping feet express "the entire spectrum of comedy, from smiles to belly laughs, into ecstatic movement." Hines earned a second Tony nomination for his performance in *Comin' Uptown.*

Hines, it seemed, was not going to be an unemployed tapper. In 1980, he appeared in the show *Black Broadway*, which traced the hits of black musicians and performers throughout the first half of the 20th century. The play's real stars, however, were the performers of the past, who included such greats as tap dancer John W. Bubbles of the famous duo Buck and Bubbles. Hines appeared with his contemporary Nell Carter (from *Ain't Misbehavin'*), and together they represented present-day black Broadway. A reviewer characterized Hines as "a one-man funky fusillade."

In February 1981, Hines opened in the Broadway smash *Sophisticated Ladies*, a revue of Duke Ellington's music. Hines exulted in his role, putting what he felt were his true talents on display for the first time. "This was *jazz!*" he proclaimed. "This was Duke Ellington! We had so much fun. . . . We jumped every night. It really was the first time I was seen by the public, the first time I really had an opportunity to do the things I can do."

Although Hines's co-star was the popular modern dancer Judith Jamison, it was Hines who won the accolades. *New York Times* critic Frank Rich wrote, "This man is human lightning and he just can't be contained." According to *New York* magazine, Hines was not only talented at dancing, singing, acting, and even drumming but was "also a redolent personality, a pervasive mood that saturates the stage with whimsy." The same reviewer declared that Hines's "tapping seems to sing even more than dance." Indeed, Hines used all his considerable talents as dancer, actor, and singer in *Sophisticated Ladies*, and he was rewarded with his third Tony nomination.

Although he loved performing in the show, Hines wanted to move on to other projects. After a year in the play, he left, and his brother, Maurice Jr. replaced him.

In 1981, during the run of *Sophisticated Ladies*, Hines and his longtime love, Pam Koslow, were married. Of their relationship, Hines has said, "This love that we have, it is the most powerful emotion in my life." He expresses his contentment and security in his marriage when he says, "I don't know what it is with Pamela and me but I am never completely comfortable when I'm not around her. . . ." Two years later, a son, Zachary, was born to the couple.

Being married to a star has its difficulties. A common question asked of celebrity spouses is whether they feel jealous that their performing spouse does love scenes with other actors—often sex symbols themselves. Koslow, for one, has said that she has "gotten used to" her husband's willingness to do love scenes in his movies and shows. Gregory is, she said, "a loving, physical man," and she acknowledged that that "is the kind of image he wants to portray to young African-American men."

A particular difficulty the couple has had to overcome is the reaction of some to an interracial marriage. Before their marriage, Pam's parents were not thrilled with the match. They came to accept their daughter's choice, however, just as Hines's own grandfather had to learn to accept Hines's mother's choice many years before.

Hines has said that in the sixties, when he was dating Pat Panella, his first wife, people on the street would occasionally stare at the racially mixed couple. Later, as social tensions loosened because of the freer attitudes of the late sixties and seventies, Hines noticed a marked change—a decrease in negative attention. As for his own feelings about his current marriage, he has said:

If someone didn't really particularly care for my choice, I have never felt that I needed to explain or justify it because my love for Pamela has always *felt* so right. From the time I met her, it just felt like we should be together. So any kind of energy that I have ever felt that people didn't particularly dig it usually passed by me pretty quickly.

Hines is hardly one for whom difficulty is an obstacle. Based on the life and career choices he has made until now, it is likely that he will do what is necessary to express himself as a person and an artist. The stubborn determination to succeed and be happy doing it appears to be one of his virtues.

Throughout the 1980s, even as Hines's career opportunities and personal life were gathering steam, he continued to perform onstage. In 1985 he began touring, and for two years, traveled and performed live as a soloist. He wanted to continue honing his dance skills. It was then that his signature style of improvisational jazz tap-dancing came into its own. "I really began to develop," he remembers, "because I sometimes had to dance every night. I was pressed to improvise. I had to come up with stuff. And I had to relax and not push."

A major problem for tap dancers is the quality of the surface on which they perform. Hines and his manager, John Shivers, attacked this never-ending problem while on tour. The two concocted a portable stage that would travel easily but still be an excellent percussive instrument. Made of oak, the floor was equipped with especially sensitive micro-phones that would pick up the sounds of Hines's feet. Since he was appearing with musicians who played electronic instruments, Hines explained that "I couldn't pound out the whole dance every night. In order to be subtle, to be able to place my foot down softly and pull it 'sh-shush,'—and still have

Hines pauses during a rehearsal to make a point. He is careful to see that his dancing, singing, and acting reflect the style he wants to project.

the audience hear it—the sound had to be loud."

Many times when performers become successful, their attitudes and behavior change, and not always for the better. Hines is aware of this and is concerned that he stay down to earth. "I'm not sure it's healthy for me to talk about myself so much," he told an interviewer. "There's so much that's unhealthy in this business. I saw it when I did *Sophisticated Ladies*. . . . 'I did this, I did that, me me me.' I'd come home and want to talk about myself some more. My wife said 'Okay, Mr. Broadway Star, take down the garbage.' And, you know, I *respected* that."

By the mid-1980s, the husband who carried out the trash *was* "Mr. Broadway Star." Gregory Hines had proved that hard work, persistence, and dedication to his craft could culminate in success. It was not just fame on Broadway, however. Hines was also proving that his talents could conquer the tough world of Hollywood.

6

THE TOUGH WORLD
OF HOLLYWOOD

HINES'S ASSERTIVENESS IS a particular necessity for black artists in the film industry. The position of minority men and women is often disturbing. With Spike Lee's successful *She's Gotta Have It* in 1986, what been a limited playing field for black film professionals began to show signs of changing. But the changes were more the result of the growth of independent filmmakers, the "indies," who usually completed and distributed their work outside the studio-controlled industry based in Hollywood. Relatively few African Americans and other minorities worked within the studio system.

Black filmmaker Oliver Micheaux, whose "independent" career spanned the decades from the 1920s through the 1940s, broke the color line fairly early in the history of movies. So too did such actors as Stepin Fetchit (the first black actor to receive star billing), Hattie McDaniel (the first black, male or female, to win an Oscar), and Bill "Bojangles" Robinson. Nevertheless, these talented entertainers were generally relegated to stereotypical roles in "white" mainstream films.

There is a story about Hattie McDaniel, who won her Oscar in 1939 for Best Supporting Actress as Scarlett O'Hara's "mammy" in *Gone with the Wind*. McDaniel often portrayed maids in films and was sometimes criticized by African Americans for

A bearded Harry Belafonte (left) and Sidney Poitier play a scene in the comedy film Buck and the Preacher. *In the exclusive world of Hollywood, Poitier and Belafonte were the exceptions as African-American actors who could garner top roles in mainstream movies.*

accepting these roles. She is said to have responded to her critics by pointing out that she could *be* a maid for seven dollars a week, or she could *play* a maid for $700 a week. She allowed as how she would rather play a maid.

Parts for blacks in films were written to appeal to a white audience, not to portray African Americans as they viewed themselves. Blacks were made to be caricatures of the way whites looked at them. Many young black filmgoers could not recognize real black people in the characters portrayed in film. An exception to this rule during the late 1940s and the 1950s is the elegant Sidney Poitier. Harry Belafonte, too, was a popular African-American film star. Other than these two talented actors, few black role models appeared in films in the post-World War II period. And when a young and impressionable Gregory Hines was tap dancing his way through nightclubs with his brother and admiring the black performers he met backstage, few African-American actors played on the big screen.

By the late 1960s, however, in the midst of the civil rights and black power movements, many African Americans criticized Poitier's roles as "sterile" or "middle class." Like young Gregory Hines, most blacks wanted portrayals more "real" and more three-dimensional than the characters Poitier portrayed.

The skyrocketing popularity of television in the 1950s and 1960s, and a corresponding decrease in movie ticket sales, threw Hollywood studios into a financial crisis. This situation, combined with the societal changes brought on by World War II and its aftermath and the black liberation movements, compelled the nearly all-white studio heads to change the film industry. It was essential to draw viewers into theaters, and black audiences were increasingly vocal in demanding more realistic portrayals of African Americans.

Gordon Parks Sr. was the first black director of a major studio film, *The Learning Tree*, for Warner Brothers Studios in 1969. Parks described the experience:

> I had fourteen or fifteen [black] people behind the camera for the first time in the history of films. There was a black director. The producer was black. The scoring was done by a black man. The third camera-man for the first time was a black man. . . . The minute [Kenny Hyman of Warner Brothers] did it, everybody felt "well, it's happened. We better open up now."

According to Parks, all it takes for change to occur is for people in positions of power in the film industry to make a commitment to diversity.

Following *The Learning Tree*, Melvin Van Peebles raised money and produced the 1970 release *Sweet Sweetback's Baad Asssss Song*. As one film historian

Brooms at the ready, Melvin Van Peebles (front) and other black actors appear in menacing roles in Sweet Sweetback's Baad Asssss Song. *Portraying African Americans as "bad black men" was the hallmark of such blaxploitation films.*

commented, Van Peebles's film singlehandedly "changed the course of African American film production and the depiction of African Americans on screen." This film, along with the films *Shaft* (1971, directed by Parks) and *Superfly* (1972, directed by Parks's son Gordon Parks Jr.), ushered in the era of "blaxploitation" films. The term, coined by the industry publication *Variety*, refers to the usually poorly made films that stereotyped blacks as aggressive, often violent, characters. However, unlike *Sweetback, Shaft,* and *Superfly*—the films that introduced the genre—later blaxploitation films were usually written, directed, and distributed by whites, who were merely exploiting an audience's need.

The idea behind blaxploitation films continued the tradition of African-American folk tales like Br'er Rabbit and John Henry, in which the hero outsmarts authority figures. Since sex, violence, and dope are often the themes of these films, they have been characterized as the "bad black man" tradition. In *Sweetback,* the main character is a hustler on the run who is protected by the black community. This was obviously a very different role from the noble characters often played by Poitier and Belafonte. The increasing visibility of African-American film professionals—on the screen and behind it—was beginning to reflect the change from white-produced films targeted to white audiences.

Despite increased exposure for black actors, blaxploitation films still represented the white view of blacks. Gregory Hines has noted that the roles for black men in blaxploitation films were just as limiting in their own way as were the earlier "sterilized" roles. Hines has consistently emphasized that African Americans must be portrayed as three-dimensional characters.

Nevertheless, even during blaxploitation's heyday in the 1970s, genuine, realistic films for black

audiences were being produced by other filmmakers, among them Harry Belafonte, Ossie Davis, and black-owned distribution companies such as TAM and Cinematics International. Sidney Poitier, too, was still a powerful influence in white Hollywood. When the era of blaxploitation films ended around 1974, these artists and companies continued to produce films that shattered the movie stereotype of African Americans.

By the time Gregory Hines broke into films in the early 1980s, Hollywood was producing yet another kind of film. While Hines was getting his career back on track, accruing Broadway credits, and starting to make films, Hollywood was discovering the "blockbuster" film. This was the age of *Star*

In an early role, Eddie Murphy (left) teamed with Richard Pryor (center) and Redd Fox in the film Harlem Nights. *They are portrayed as affable gangsters who in the end do the right thing, making the film a step above the standard blaxploitation movie.*

Hines shares a quiet moment with Loretta Devine who plays his love interest, Gloria, in the 1995 film Waiting to Exhale. *The movie exemplifies the changing trend from "lily-white" Hollywood films to films featuring African Americans.*

Wars, Jaws, and *Indiana Jones.* Rather than make unique films that appeal to selected audiences, Hollywood invested monumental sums of money in films calculated to have the widest possible audience appeal. Again, African-American film professionals found that they were mostly ignored by Hollywood. Richard Pryor and Eddie Murphy did become superstars in white-produced, mostly white-cast films, pulling in a sizable African-American audience. Aside from these two stars, however, Hollywood still offered few opportunities for blacks.

It is essential, says Gregory Hines, particularly for black artists, to be aggressive in going after what they want. He has never shied away from aggressively pursuing his film goals. Describing how he got the role in the 1986 film *Running Scared*, he explained his method:

> I read the script, and I knew it was a good part. It was written for a white actor. That's what I'm up against— I have to try to make roles happen for me that aren't written black. The roles written black are the 'cool guys,' and I don't want to play the cool guy. . . . It's incumbent upon me to go after things, because nobody's going to say "Why are we just looking at white actors? Let's look at everybody." They never do that. . . .

Although many film professionals feel that the lack of obvious opportunities for minorities is the result and perpetuation of racism in America, it is important to note that the film industry is a business—Hollywood needs to make money. The budgets for blockbuster films, including mass marketing strategies, were and are so enormous that the films *must* draw in as many people as possible just for the studio to break even, let alone make a profit. And without profits, studios are even less willing than usual to consider producing modest projects that appeal to smaller audiences—and thus bring in lower profits. Films targeted to a mass audience simply take into account the fact that most of that audience is white.

Yaphet Kotto, a black actor who has played significant roles in Hollywood-produced films, agrees, concluding that the situation is based on economics, not racism. "People want to be involved in fifteen- to twenty-million-dollar movies, and they want their returns guaranteed," he said. "So they go for the Redfords, the Connerys, the Brandos . . . if they ever scale their expectations down and return to modest, low-budget films, they might just turn to me."

Whatever the reason, the statistics show that Hollywood has traditionally been closed to all but a very few minority men and women. In 1969, 40 percent of the Los Angeles metropolitan area population was minorities. But minorities comprised only three percent of the film industry's labor force. In the 1980s, the situation remained largely unchanged. Litigation and the threat of a boycott by the NAACP and other organizations exposed the fact that very few minorities—especially minority women—were being hired at the major studios. Only one-tenth of the 50 black-directed theatrical films were done by women, and the first was in 1991 (*Daughters in the Dust*, directed by Julie Dash). In 1991, out of 450 studio and major independent releases, only 12 were directed by black men and none by black women. (Dash produced and released her film completely outside the studio system.)

Film industry insiders claim that getting jobs in the film industry depends on "who you know." Since nearly all of the power positions in Hollywood are still held by white males, it is their white male acquaintances and business associates who are more likely than minorities to get a foot in the door. Minorities are then at a disadvantage because they do not hear about potential jobs in a word-of-mouth recruiting system. Gregory Hines is quite aware of this system. He himself has been cast in shows in which he knew the producer, director, or another influential person–for example, *Wolfen* and *Running Scared*.

Still, several successful films released in the 1990s and featuring story lines relevant to the African-American experience have proved that there is an audience demand for films that are not all "lily-white." Movies such as *The Preacher's Wife, A Rage in Harlem*, and *Waiting to Exhale* (all of which Hines appeared in) have proved to Hollywood that profits can be made by increasing minority roles in films.

Hines himself believes things are changing, as he explained: "Besides developing roles for black actors, producers and directors are starting to realize, Hey, we don't have to write 'black' dialogue; just hire a black actor and say, 'Make it *you*.' The day is gone when every black man has to be 'Yeah, man, I dig it.' I mean, black people also say, 'Yes, I understand.'"

Hines's own film career is proof of his belief. Any artist as talented and determined as Hines is bound to break out of the expected track and forge his own career—whether on stage, in films, or in television.

7

GREGORY HINES,
MOVIE STAR

———— ❧ ————

UNLIKE HIS FIRST break into Broadway, Hines's early film auditions were anything but romantic movie material. "I read for a basketball movie called *The Fish That Saved Pittsburgh,* and a movie that was never released called *House of God* that Howard Rollins was in," he recalled. Despite being rejected, the aspiring film actor stuck with it, however, knowing it was something he was eager to try.

Gregory had also had some encouragement from another highly regarded actor. Before he had dropped out and gone to California, Hines had been spotted by Dustin Hoffman during one of his gigs at the Plaza Hotel's Persian Room in New York City. At that time Hoffman encouraged Hines to seek a film career, telling the dancer he thought he had ability as an actor.

Nothing comes easily, however. In show business much of a person's success or lack of it has to do with timing. About two years after the Persian Room meeting, when Hoffman was looking for Hines for a film project, the dancer was in Venice, California, out of show business for the time being.

Once Hines was back in the entertainment field, he knew that film was something he wanted to try. "I wanted to make a movie," Hines says. "The whole life of the movies appealed to me. You work hard for

In the explosive opening scene of his 1989 film Tap, *Hines dances feverishly in his prison cell, expressing his rage and frustration at himself for abandoning the world of tap for a life of crime.*

three or four months, then you don't work at all for a couple of months. I also like the idea of doing a movie, then doing a play, couple of movies, then a play. Also, if you do a movie, you can go see it."

Doing live stage work is transient, something dancers and stage actors must get used to; seeing one's own work is a treat. "I love it," he said of making movies. "I love the environment. I love the collaborative excitement. And I love making something that can last. Most of my life I have been doing things that, once done, they disappear."

In 1981, as Hines was getting used to consistent work on Broadway and was building a life with his new wife, the beginnings of a film career opened up. He was tapped for a role in the film *Wolfen*, whose lead was Albert Finney. About his film debut, Hines said that it was "the first time I ever did any kind of a [show business] job where I didn't dance."

Although Hines may have missed a chance to work with Dustin Hoffman by being out of circulation, he had important connections. His first film role, as a medical examiner in *Wolfen*, came to him in part because he knew the film's director "from when we were hippies together." Talent and skill are not the same thing, however. Hines still had to learn to *act*. He has described how it worked:

> I think sometimes Albert [Finney] would just *look* at me—just before we would have to go through a doorway, when the cameras were running—and realize I had nothing on my mind except the words I was trying to remember. Sometimes he would just suggest something: "If I were you, I would want to be a little somber when I came through that door." And suddenly a light bulb would go off in my head—he would make the words *mean* something.

Although Hines did not make it to the end of the film (he was devoured by wolves halfway through), he obviously learned a great deal about acting from the experience. And his aptitude for the craft has

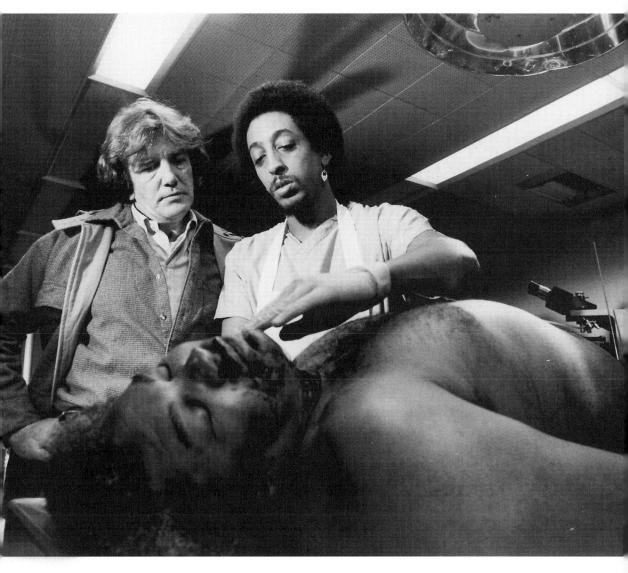

only increased with practice. Over the years Hines's development as an actor has contributed greatly to his attractiveness as a "property," encouraging producers and directors to cast him in nondancing as well as dancing roles. His star power also helps assure backing. As a well-known talent, his name on a project can command financing. After years of work, Hines is probably best known as an actor by his many new fans.

With Albert Finney in the horror thriller Wolfen, *Hines plays a medical examiner. The film was not a box-office success, but it did give him a chance to work with a major actor and hone his own acting skills.*

It is not just Hines's acting skills that are in demand for films, however. In the 1984 film *The Cotton Club*, he meshed his dancing skills with his talent as an actor. In the film, Gregory portrayed tap dancer William Sandman, one-half of a tapping duo. His brother, Maurice Jr., was cast as his partner. Hines characterized *The Cotton Club* as "The big return of dance to the screen. . . . It was only a matter of time before people would want to see dance in movies." Unlike other dance films, such as *Flashdance, Saturday Night Fever,* and *Dirty Dancing*, however, *The Cotton Club* was a film about old-fashioned tap dancing. The film's director, Francis Ford Coppola, assembled an impressive cast of tap dancers, which included Henry LeTang and Charles "Honi" Coles, the legendary soft-shoe tapper.

Hines particularly liked working with Coppola. The director did thorough research, going through endless period footage of tap dancing, and carefully videotaped all rehearsals. Yet Coppola also improvised, an approach that strongly appealed to Hines. "He [Coppola] sets up situations," Hines explained, "then lets you improvise. He's like a jazz musician, he's so sensitive."

In *The Cotton Club*, Gregory's character, William, breaks up the act with his brother, as Hines did in real life. And, in real life, the two brothers were no longer close. Gregory attributes much of this to the fact that he and Maurice are very different. He also blames sibling rivalry because they are both in the same profession. "So much of our relationship was the act," Gregory explains. "And maybe with my brother and me, the act might have been what kept us together. And when it was gone, it was tough for us to find a reason to spend time together."

Maurice sees their relationship somewhat differently. He certainly acknowledges that Gregory is immensely talented but adds that his brother "knows how to play the system." He criticizes Gregory for

roles he has played in black revues. Maurice insists that his true interest lies in the legitimate theater and not in redoing black shows. Maurice also con-tends that his brother compromises. He reinforces his point by citing a role Gregory played in the Mel Brooks film *History of the World, Part I* in which he portrayed a slave. That, says Maurice, is a part he would never accept.

Despite the antagonisms, when Hines was asked what he thought of the experience of filming *The Cotton Club*, he replied, "I loved it." Pam Koslow

In a scene from The Cotton Club, *Hines hoofs it with a bevy of chorus girls. The Cotton Club gave the multitalented performer his first chance to show on film all the things he could do.*

Making The Cotton Club *was a reunion for Gregory and Maurice Jr., seen here in a scene from the film. It also proved to be a wrenching experience as the brothers reenacted their own real-life split-up.*

remembered things differently, however. "It was the worst. The tension was real thick most of the time." Problems were particularly evident during filming of the breakup scene. Hines recalled that "things were still tense from when I left. . . . That was very painful for Maurice—he wasn't ready to break up the act."

Playing the scene was painful for both brothers. In one day, they had to replay their splitting up at least eight times. Coppola was expert at getting them to relive the experience. "For a while, we were *yelling* at each other," Gregory says. "And Francis just said,

'Oh, good, thank you.'" When the scene was finally finished, Gregory and Maurice were crying, as were their parents, who were on the set that day.

The conflict between Gregory and Maurice was not the only behind-the-scenes drama. One was how Gregory got the part to begin with. The original director, Robert Evans, wanted Hines for the part of Cab Calloway and Richard Pryor for the role of Sandman Williams. Hines insisted on seeing the script, which Evans was keeping a secret. According to Hines, he sneaked a draft of the script out of Evans's office and read it. He definitely did not want the part of Calloway; he wanted the main part.

When he confronted Evans, they had a monumental argument, and Evans flatly refused. At that point, Hines relates, "I instituted a reign of terror on Robert Evans. I called him every day. I went over to his house twice again, uninvited. It got to the point where he was actually yelling at me over the phone, 'Stop calling me! I know you want the part.'"

Hines admits he was extremely aggressive, although he denies he was obnoxious. "Well, I got close on that one," he does admit. But he got the role he wanted, playing the character William Sandman. Other difficulties with *The Cotton Club* included an unfinished script when shooting began. When a final script did appear and actors were dissatisfied with it, director Coppola kept working on it. He handed out fresh pages nearly every day of shooting, in what one actor called "a most unorthodox film experience."

Such a filming experience might put off many actors, but Hines felt he had a lot of creative room in which to maneuver. Richard Gere was the star, and his name had attracted much of the financing; therefore his role was primary. It was Hines, however, who persisted with Coppola to help create a black story line.

Hines's co-star, Lonette McKee, whose character had only five lines of dialogue in the script's early draft, remembers that Hines told her, "Don't get put off by the cheesy part. We're gonna be right up there with Richard and Diane [Lane], but what we've got to do is help Francis create." McKee laughed, "He was probably just saying that for moral support, but I'll tell you, [the black story line] was not there when we walked in."

When the project started, Hines appreciated the film as one that could present a positive image for young African Americans. He also had a personal interest as well, since his grandmother Ora had been a showgirl at the real Cotton Club. Hines also had fond memories of playing in a Cotton Club revue in Miami when he was only 11. He appeared then with Cab Calloway, who told the young tapper about the real Cotton Club and its famous entertainers. Undoubtedly the legend of the real Cotton Club contributed to Hines's eagerness to play a prominent part in the film and make it a movie that, he said, "black people could be proud of—something that would show them as *special*."

In 1985, Hines again displayed his formidable dancing skills in the critically acclaimed film *White Nights*, a thriller set in the former Soviet Union. (The title refers to the long daylight periods that occur during the summer in northern Russia.) Hines plays Raymond Greenwood, an American dancer who defects to the Soviet Union to protest the racism of the draft during the Vietnam War. He stars opposite the legendary ballet dancer Mikhail Baryshnikov who, as Kolya Rodchenko, relives part of Baryshnikov's own real life as a defector to the United States. Director Taylor Hackford freely admits blending fact and fiction by drawing on the two artists' personal experiences in creating their characters.

In a plot that often twists and turns, Kolya, who has defected, returns to the Soviet Union. He is nabbed by the secret police and forced to stay with Greenwood and his wife (played by Isabella Rossellini)

in a sumptuous apartment in Leningrad (now St. Petersburg). Greenwood is supposed to try and persuade Kolya to remain in the Soviet Union. As the plot develops, Greenwood, now wanting to return to the United States, and Kolya attempt to escape, which gives the actors plenty of action and lively "thriller" scenes.

The plot, however, is only a device to display the incredible dancing of Hines and Baryshnikov. Nine

Hines and Mikhail Baryshinikov soar in a dancing duet in the film White Nights. *In addition to his dancing, Hines added a meaty dramatic role to his credits.*

dance numbers include an intense and stirring solo by Baryshnikov, who expresses his anger and frustration at his nation's dreary oppression. In one scene Hines, as Greenwood, half speaks and half taps the story of his struggle as a young dancer and his disillusionment with the American establishment.

What surprised critics were the dramatic talents of the film's stars. Baryshnikov's acting skills were virtually untested. And although Hines was well known for his dancing roles, his film credits had not established him as a leading dramatic actor. Both succeeded in bringing what one writer called "genuine emotion" to their parts. Hines was impressed with his co-star. "He was acting while he was dancing," he exclaimed. "I thought, 'That is what I want to do. I want to speak of anger, frustration, insecurity, jealousy in my dancing.'"

Hines's character also challenged the popular view of black tap dancers as "novelty acts," versus the view of ballet dancers as artists. Hackford explained the film's concept: "What I was trying to do was get at the root of what the frustration of their lives as artists has been. . . . I think it's a real feeling that Greg had, and he was able to express it."

For the 1986 film *Running Scared,* Hines did not have to challenge anyone's view of dance. In fact, he did not dance at all in the film. With co-star Billy Crystal, he plays a Chicago undercover cop who, with his partner, wants to retire. For both Hines and Crystal, these were their first roles as leading men. The film was not a great dramatic epic; rather, it gave Hines a crack at comedy and what one writer called "a finger-snapping style . . . that makes the whole thing click."

Both actors had to work out vigorously to build up some muscle. Crystal remarked with his usual wit, "Once we read the script and knew we had to take our shirts off on page 62, we started to pump. Gregory is built like a greyhound, and when he started, he was very skinny." But Hines channels his assertiveness in whatever direction it needs to go. According to Crystal, ". . . he attacks things. The day after we began working out, he had a body-building book and magazines like *You and Your Tendons* and *The Wonderful World of Thighs*." If there was any question of Hines's talent or ability as a leading man, director Peter Hyams laid it to rest: "In terms of talent, Gregory is an absolute thermonuclear weapon just waiting to go off."

A major challenge for Hines in his pursuit of a film career has been the stereotypical views of tap dancing. Since the 1930s, when Fred Astaire and his elegant co-stars (including Ginger Rogers) distracted Americans from the Great Depression with formal top hats and tails and fabulous evening gowns, few films have portrayed tap dancing. For Hines, who wanted a film career but saw himself primarily as a tap dancer, combining the two art forms of dance and film as well as overcoming racial prejudice was a huge job—but has proven a successful one.

In 1989 Hines got the chance to star in a film that not only showcased his dancing and acting talents but also presented the personal story of a tap dancer named Max Washington. The movie, *Tap,* also tells the story of some legendary tappers who continued dancing even when tap dancing was out of style. These dancers play themselves. Among the tappers who appeared were "Sandman" Sims, Jimmy Slyde, Bunny Briggs, Arthur Duncan, Harold Nicholas, Steve Condos, and Pat Rico. Hines was especially drawn to the film because, as he said, "The charm of this movie is that these are the real people who lived the parts they are playing. Everyone connected with this film has their whole lifetime in it."

Hines plays Max Washington, a tap dancer and the son of a great tap dancer who has turned to the more lucrative business of crime when dancing as a career dries up. Returning from prison, Max is discouraged and saddened because he has abandoned

In a highly charged scene from Tap, Hines engages in a tapping challenge with his co-stars, the tap-dancing veterans who played themselves in the film.

his life as a dancer and feels there is no place for him to go. With the urging and encouragement of his girlfriend, Amy, and her father, Little Mo, played by one of Hines's idols, Sammy Davis Jr., Max re-enters the world of tap dancing. He salvages his career when he and Little Mo create an entirely new style of dancing.

The film's director, Nick Castle Jr., is the son of a noted tap dancer and choreographer who worked with film's tap greats in the 1930s and 1940s. Choreographer Henry LeTang also worked on the film. In addition, the film stars a young Chance Taylor and a very young Savion Glover, the tap sensation who appeared in *Jelly's Last Jam* and went on to raves in the show *Bring in 'Da Noise, Bring in 'Da Funk.*

Far from being nostalgic, *Tap* explores the reasons for the decline of tap dancing and its revival as a dance form. Indeed, half of the film is devoted to bringing tap into a modern, urban setting. The film was not a huge commercial success. It did, however, bring to the big screen the story of tap dancing in the last half of the 20th century. And it showcased three generations of tap dancers in a lively story line that engages its audience.

Gregory Hines's personality has been a great asset in advancing his career in films. His director on *Running Scared* characterized him as a person with an "enormous wellspring of warmth. He's a real hugger, a kisser. I wanted that affectionate quality for the character." And co-star Billy Crystal also praises Hines's personal character: "Gregory is the kindest person I've ever seen with people. He's totally unselfish." So whatever Hines's aggressiveness accomplishes for his career, he balances it with an affable personality that has undoubtedly made him many friends in the film industry.

8

WHAT'S NEXT?

———— ❦ ————

DURING HIS PHENOMENAL career, Gregory Hines has performed as dancer, actor, and singer. Yet he still remains essentially a tap dancer. "It's the way I communicate best," he has said. Where does he think tap dancing as a medium of expression is headed? In the late 1980s, he expressed his ideas about tap, explaining that the conventional image of a tap dancer as a slight person decked out in tails or tuxedo had to be shaken up. He pointed out that people are attracted to ballet and modern dance because they see beautiful, expressive bodies that are not swathed in clothing. Certainly Hines has been instrumental in changing this image of the tap dancer and modernizing it to appeal to new, young audiences.

Hines believes that tap dancing, long considered a form of entertainment but not of art, must "defend its choreographic integrity . . . particularly on the Broadway scene." He noted that in the 1980s most Broadway chorus tap dancing was created by choreographers who knew little about tap. They put together some basic steps, he explained, and tossed in some ballet. It pleased audiences, but it was not dazzling tap dancing.

There can be no doubt that in the 1990s the situation is definitely changing for the better. Hines felt very strongly—and still feels—that a solid base of talent is available to take tap to new heights. And he

Whatever comes next for Gregory Hines, he has secured his place in the entertainment business as a person of many talents who has also been a major innovator in changing the world of tap dancing.

strongly urges using that talent instead of encouraging mediocre performances by people who are not primarily tap dancers. He described his ideas: "Our creative abilities can take wing because we have the people who can do the stuff. When we saw that group, that ensemble, tap dancing in the amazing way that we have seen in great ballet and great modern dance—it would have an impact."

When asked about his young friend and protégé Savion Glover, whom Hines refers to with affection as "The Man," Hines concedes that Savion and other young dancers today are more technically skilled at tap than even he is. Savion is tap's "wonder boy," Hines says, and describes the young dancer's style:

> You know, I've tried many times to steal some of Jimmy Slyde's stuff and I *can't* get it. . . . But Savion can do Jimmy Slyde. He can do Buster Brown. He can do me and anything that Henry LeTang gives him. What's going to happen in five years, when this kid evolves into *Savion?* He'll have a sense of us inside him—and he'll be doing what nobody is doing. *He* is where tap dance is going.

Savion Glover has had a phenomenal influence on the development and popularity of tap. At age 11, Glover starred in the hit Broadway show and Tony Award–winning *The Tap Dance Kid*. He appeared in the 1989 film *Tap* with Hines and Sammy Davis Jr., and again with Gregory Hines in *Jelly's Last Jam*, for which he won a Drama Desk Award for best actor. Glover has also appeared on *Sesame Street*, where he can still be seen in reruns, and at the 1996 Academy Awards, where he danced a tribute to the late Gene Kelly.

This extraordinarily talented young man also choreographed and starred in the hit Broadway show and tap phenomenon *Bring in 'Da Noise, Bring in 'Da Funk*, which earned no less than *nine* Tony nominations. The show highlights the history of African-American dance in a Broadway musical style. Glover won the 1991 Martin Luther King Jr. Outstanding Youth Award and the 1996 *Dance Magazine* Award—the youngest recipient ever. If anyone can bring tap into the new millennium, it is Savion Glover.

In addition to *Noise/Funk,* several other shows have rocked the dance world by incorporating new elements into the traditional artistry of syncopated dance. *Tap Dogs,* created by Australian steelworkers; *Stomp,* performed by a troupe of English stage actors; and Michael Flatley's lightning-speed Irish dancing in *Riverdance* and *Lord of the Dance* have all spread the popularity of the dance form to almost unprecedented levels. "We did a study and were just overwhelmed by the diversity of the audience . . . it's the full range of people from 5 to 95," Michael Flatley notes.

These new dance shows that are sweeping the performance world have several aspects in common—including elements that Gregory Hines predicted would help modernize tap and spread it to new audiences. The beauty of bodies is one factor. "These acts exude a different kind of sexiness from ballet or other forms of dance," says one reviewer, "the kind you get when a rock singer takes off his shirt." How much further from a stereotypical tapper in a tuxedo can you get?

These shows also include a rock-and-roll spirit, which appeals to younger audiences. *Lord of the Dance* in particular uses light shows and other elements of rock concerts to wow its audiences. Music critics have noted that tap can easily incorporate hip-hop and rap, encouraging young dancers to tap dance to contemporary music.

The new styles also display an athletic spirit that has often been missing from dance in the past. Previously, the goal of many kinds of performance dance had been to mask the difficulty—to make the dancing appear effortless. Now, the hip style is to let the audience see the athleticism and effort it takes to perform new dance styles, lending the entire performance a raw power and energy.

The percussive sounds of tap, particularly in the show *Stomp*, take on a new style. The group uses trash cans, sticks, car keys, and brooms, among other objects, to create an irresistible rhythm—with practically no accompanying music. *Tap Dogs* too uses only the sound of steelworkers' boots hitting the stage floor.

One last element completes the stew. It is what theater critic Lawson Taitte calls "working-class chic." These performers—Michael Flatley, Savion Glover, and Sheldon and Dein Perry of *Tap Dogs*—make no secret of their working-class origins and, in some cases, capitalize on it. In *Tap Dogs*, the cast wears jeans and steelworkers' boots and welds the set together. The performers in *Stomp* are depicted as janitors. With their aura of ordinariness, combined with brilliant talent, the appeal of these shows is nearly irresistible to the average man, woman, or kid. Just as Hines predicted, audiences are dazzled.

What does the resurgent popularity of tap dancing, in all its glorious new forms, mean for Gregory Hines? It should mean that his continuing career in dance is assured. All dancers age, however. Hines has always been aware that the day will come when he won't be able to dance professionally: "Skill diminishes with age; it's just mathematics," he concedes. Nevertheless, he faces the day with a positive attitude as he refers to a fellow performer: "Like Nipsey Russell said, 'I'm not as good as I once was, but I'm as good once as I ever was.'"

Hines knows from rough experience that the wear and tear of performing on Broadway will one day be too much for him, perhaps sooner than he thinks. This is, and has always been, one of his reasons for pursuing a film career. "Three or four musical films

Hines and Tommy Tune tap out a routine in preparation for the PBS Great Performances program Gregory Hines: Tap Dance in America, *one of the many television specials in which Hines has appeared.*

Hines's versatility as an actor is reflected in the many different roles he has played on the big screen. Here, in a scene from The Preacher's Wife, Hines (center), as businessman Joe Hamilton, shows Reverend Henry Biggs, played by Courtney B. Vance (left), plans he has drawn up for the preacher's new church.

[a year] is easier than eight Broadway shows a week," he said, and went on to explain:

There are steps I could do in film all day that I couldn't do eight shows a week. Gene Kelly and Fred Astaire would do steps for 40 seconds or a minute and a half on film, and then 'Cut! Break!' That's how they stayed so young. Jimmy Slyde is dancing and he's in his mid-fifties, and Bunny Briggs, who's in his early sixties. They can still do sixteenth notes! I want to carry on their legacy—so that one day it will be Jelly's Last Jam with Savion Glover, featuring Gregory Hines as the Chimney Man. I'm going to tap-dance until I can't!

Professional entertainers are wise to ensure their futures. Diversifying their sources of income is one excellent way to do it. Gregory Hines, with his multitude of talents, seems to have little to worry about in that regard. He could undoubtedly have a successful singing career. As early as 1987, he made a single with Luther Vandross called "There's Nothing Better Than Love." The song immediately went to Number 1 on *Billboard's Black Singles* chart. A year later, he became a recording artist with Epic Records and launched his debut album, *Gregory Hines*. He sang eight songs, including "Love Don't Love You Anymore," "This Is What I Believe," and "I'm Gonna Get to You."

Gregory Hines has also been incredibly successful in other arenas as well. Throughout the 1980s and 1990s, while appearing in films and on Broadway, he was also keeping a hectic schedule of television appearances and special shows. He has made television movies, including *Louisiana Black, T Bone 'N Weasel, A Stranger in Town,* and *The Cherokee Kid.* In 1996 he appeared in the charming Hollywood comedy *The Preacher's Wife*, along with Denzel Washington, Whitney Houston, and Courtney B. Vance. In the film, he plays the role of a real-estate tycoon named Joe Hamilton who is going to help the Reverend Henry Biggs, played by Courtney B. Vance, build a new church.

Hines has been part of numerous television specials: participating in a birthday tribute to South Africa's president Nelson Mandela, sharing in a celebration of the performing arts from the Kennedy Center in Washington, D.C., hosting The 16th Annual Black Filmmakers Hall of Fame, and performing in the PBS special *Gregory Hines: Tap Dance in America*, for which he won an Emmy Award.

Hines also appeared on *Saturday Night Live (SNL)* with legendary pianist Eubie Blake in what was one of the most acclaimed of that program's shows. It took some doing to get on the popular

Hines hugs his television son, played by Brandon Hammond, in a scene from his own Gregory Hines Show. *Despite his affectionate, warm portrayal, the show ran for only one season.*

show, but Hines displayed the same boldness he had shown in getting his role in *The Cotton Club.* He went to *SNL* producer's office and claimed he had an appointment, which was not true. He waited for a time and finally left when he realized the producer was letting him sit and wait. Back the next day, he told the same story to a secretary, insisting he had an appointment. When she told that he was indeed in the appointment book, Hines was somewhat taken aback. "What? I am?" he exclaimed. He quickly recovered, however. "Obviously he'd told her if I came back he'd see me," Hines said.

Hines also made his debut as a director in 1994 with the film *White Man's Burden*. Shot in New York City, the movie is about the relationship between a black high-school girl and her 30-year-old white lover. Hines said he was intrigued by the idea of the culture and age difference between the black young woman and the older white man.

In 1997 Hines finally participated in a project he has held close to his heart for years. *The Gregory Hines Show* premiered on September 15, 1997. Certainly the show helped eliminate the dearth of prime-time African-American-oriented shows airing on major television networks. It also contributed its own intelligence to the family-comedy scene. Unfortunately for Hines and his fans the show was canceled in the spring of 1998, after only 16 episodes.

Reviewers, however, were enthusiastic about the show. Hines played Ben Stevenson, a single father in his forties. Brandon Hammond was Ben's 12-year-old son, and Bill Cobbs co-starred as Ben's father. One reviewer wrote that "The chemistry between Hammond and Hines is amazing, and their affectionate relationship feels real, and is quite touching. Hines is one of the most charismatic actors working today, and I'm glad to see him in something that does his talent justice."

For a man whose talents seem nearly limitless— tap dancer, actor, singer, drummer—what else can Gregory Hines do? It seems the question is, rather, what *can't* he do? Which talent is closest to his heart, however? According to Hines, the stage is his first love. "My roots in show business come from the live stage and that's where I belong," he responds. "My style is part choreography, part improvisation. That gives me a chance to show people the possibilities of tap dancing, which, at its heart, is mathematics with endless possibilities."

When Hines is not performing or rehearsing or planning his next project, he lives in New York City's Greenwich Village, where until recently he

Hines has always had a special place for his family, despite disruptions in their relationships. Here he is joined by his father and young son along with, from left to right, Pamela's daughter, Jessica, Pamela, and daughter Daria.

had shared a duplex with Pam and their son, Zachary. Daria is married. His current apartment is equipped with a hot tub, an entertainment center, and a darkroom, where he develops his own film. Despite the childhood injury to his eye, Hines is an avid photographer. He works almost exclusively in black and white portraits and photographs only people he knows and with whom he feels comfortable.

Gregory also lifts weights to keep in shape, and he enjoys watching football games. As a boy he was a pretty good football player. "I wanted to play football," he has said. "I wanted to follow that dream.

Sometimes when I watch football games, I sit and dream to myself, 'Gee, if I had played football'. . . . That's the one thing I think about when I think of an alternative [career]."

Sometimes Hines just likes to break out into tapping to express his energy and exuberance. Where does he really like to tap privately? In elevators. He told an interviewer: "For some reason, if I can get into an elevator and there's nobody else with me, there's a nice little boom and slap sound. . . . I've been able to come up with some really good steps in elevators, and later on I try to remember them."

What does Gregory Hines want to be remembered for? He does not have a problem explaining. "Oh, that's easy. I would like to be remembered with love by my family and friends, the people who really know me. When it all comes down to it, that's what's important in life. I never think in terms of anyone else remembering me—that would just be icing on the cake."

Hines's devotion to his family and close friends continues despite his separation from Pam Koslow, announced in early 1998. Hines's publicist, who announced the split, emphasized that the couple is not divorcing. Time will tell whether the two, who have been together for more than 20 years, will reunite.

Life—and work—goes on for Mr. Human Lightning. Gregory Hines realizes, however, that as dear to him as his talents are, they will not last forever, and no one, however talented, can afford to neglect the most important parts of life.

> Sometimes when I think about the whole scheme of things, I think that being a parent is really why I'm here. Not to tap dance or entertain, but to love my children and teach them how to love so that they can love their children and the cycle is unbroken. That's why I get chills just thinking about a grandchild—that I would be able to hold a child that comes from my child and know that my child can love this baby because I was able to love her because my parents love me. *That's* what it's all about.

CHRONOLOGY

1946 Born to Alma and Maurice Hines on February 14 in New York City

1949 Begins learning tap steps from brother, Maurice Jr.

1952 Begins performing professionally with brother as the Hines Kids

1954 Hines Kids perform at Harlem's Apollo Theater

1962 Hines Kids tour nightclub circuit in U.S.; appear on television (*Ed Sullivan Show*, *Jackie Gleason Show*); perform in Europe

1963 Maurice Sr. joins the act and the name is changed to Hines, Hines and Dad; tour U.S. and Europe; appear on *The Tonight Show* with Johnny Carson

1968 Marries Patricia Panella and settles in New York City

1971 Daughter, Daria, born

1973 Leaves Hines, Hines and Dad, and moves to Venice, California

1974–7 Leads hippie lifestyle; founds jazz-rock band; writes unsuccessful songs; works as busboy and teaches karate; is divorced from Patricia Panella; meets future wife Pamela Koslow

1978 Returns to New York City; lands role on Broadway in *The Last Minstrel Show*; appears in show *Eubie* and is nominated for a Tony Award

1979 Appears in musical *Comin' Uptown* and is nominated for second Tony

1981 Marries Pamela Koslow; stars in *Sophisticated Ladies* and is nominated for third Tony; makes film debut in *Wolfen* with Albert Finney

1982 Tours U.S. with *Sophisticated Ladies*

1984 Stars in film *The Cotton Club* with brother Maurice Jr.

1985 Films *White Nights* with Mikhail Baryshnikov; appears in PBS special *About Tap*; begins touring as a soloist

1986 Films *Running Scared* with Billy Crystal

1987 Records first single "There's Nothing Better Than Love", which hits Number 1 on *Black Singles* chart; performs onstage in *Jazz Tap Ensemble*

1988 Performs *An Evening of Tap* onstage; records album *Gregory Hines*; films *Off Limits* with Willem Dafoe

1988	Plays Feste the Clown in *Twelfth Night*; stars in film *Tap*; appears in PBS special *Gregory Hines: Tap in America*, which wins Emmy Award
1991	Films *Eve of Destruction* and *A Rage in Harlem*
1992	Stars in *Jelly's Last Jam*; wins Tony Award for Best Actor in a Musical; appears in PBS special *Jammin': Jelly Roll Morton on Broadway*
1994	Directs film *White Man's Burden*
1995	Stars in television movie *A Stranger in Town*; films *Waiting to Exhale*
1996	Films *Good Luck, Mad Dog Time*, and *The Preacher's Wife*
1998	Produces and stars in television series *The Gregory Hines Show*; canceled in 1998; films *The Tic Code*
1999	Films *Once in the Life*

ACCOMPLISHMENTS

ALBUM

1988   *Gregory Hines*

FILMS

1981   *History of the World, Part I*

            Wolfen

1983   *Deal of the Century*

1984   *The Cotton Club*

            The Muppets Take Manhattan

1985   *White Nights*

1986   *Running Scared*

1988   *Off Limits*

1989   *Tap*

1991   *Eve of Destruction*

            A Rage in Harlem

            White Lie (also called *Louisiana Black*, TV movie)

1992   *T Bone 'N Weasel* (TV movie)

1994   *Dead Air* (TV movie)

            Kangaroo Court

            Renaissance Man

            White Man's Burden (Directed)

1995   *A Stranger in Town* (TV movie)

            Waiting to Exhale

1996   *The Cherokee Kid* (TV movie)

            Good Luck

            Mad Dog Time

            The Preacher's Wife

1997   *Color of Justice* (TV movie)

MUSICALS AND STAGE PERFORMANCES

TELEVISION SHOWS AND APPEARANCES

1988	*Freedomfest: Nelson Mandela's 70th Birthday Celebration*
	Dionne Warwick in London (syndicator)
	The 42nd Annual Tony Awards
1989	*Gregory Hines: Tap Dance in America* (Also called *Dance in America*)
1989	*The 61st Annual Academy Awards Presentation*
	The 21st Annual NAACP Image Awards
	The 16th Annual Black Filmmakers Hall of Fame (syndicator, host)
1990	*The Stellar Gospel Music Awards* (syndicator)
	Sammy Davis Jr.'s 60th Anniversary Celebration
1991	*The Kennedy Center Honors: A Celebration of the Performing Arts*
	The Dancing Man—Peg Leg Bates
1992	*Jammin': Jelly Roll Morton on Broadway* (also choreographed)
1994	*Baseball* (miniseries, voice)
1997	*Subway Stories: Tales from the Underground*
1997–8	*The Gregory Hines Show*

FURTHER READING

"Baryshnikov and Hines in *White Nights*." *Dance Magazine*, November 1985.

Blum, David. "Hollywood Shakespeare: Joe Papp Sprinkles Stardust on *Twelfth Night*." *New York*, June 19, 1989.

Bogle, Donald. *Blacks in American Film and Television*. New York: Garland, 1988.

———. *Toms, Coons, Mulattoes, Mammies and Bucks*. New York: Continuum, 1991.

Charleston, Rita. "Gregory Hines Is Going Non-Stop." *The Philadelphia Tribune*, July 19, 1996.

"Comin' Uptown." *New York*, January 14, 1980.

Coombs, Orde. "Gregory Hines Taps to the Top." *New York*, March 30, 1981.

Frank, Rusty E. *Tap! The Greatest Tap Dance Stars and Their Stories*. Foreword by Gregory Hines. Revised edition. New York: Da Capo Press, 1994.

Gill, Brendan. *"Comin' Uptown." New Yorker*, January 7, 1980.

———. *"Eubie!" New Yorker*, October 2, 1978.

Graustark, Barbara. "Tapped for Stardom." *American Film*, December 1984.

"Gregory Hines." Lazar Productions, 1995.

Guerrero, Ed. *Framing Blackness: The African American Image in Film*. Philadelphia: Temple University Press, 1993.

Kael, Pauline. "The Current Cinema." *New Yorker*, June 29, 1981. Jan. 7, 1985. Nov. 18, 1985.

Kroll, Jack. *"Jelly's Last Jam." Newsweek*, May 4, 1992.

Norment, Lynn. "Gregory Hines: Dancer Wins Stardom as Chicago Vice Cop." *Ebony*, October 1986.

Null, Gary. *Black Hollywood: The Black Performer in Motion Pictures*. New York: Citadel Press, 1975.

O'Donnell, Maureen. "The Origins of Art Lie in Diversity and Oppression." *Chicago Sun-Times*, July 7, 1998.

Porterfield, Christopher. "Black Broadway." *Time*, May 19, 1980.

Randolph, Laura. "Gregory Hines on Fame, Family and His Years of Living Dangerously." *Ebony*, January 1991.

Randolph, Laura. *"Jelly's Last Jam* and the Pain and Passion of Gregory Hines." *Ebony*, September 1992.

Rhines, Jesse Algeron. *Black Film/White Money*. New Brunswick, NY: Rutgers University Press, 1996.

Smith, Dinitia. "Jelly on a Roll." *New York*, June 8, 1992.

Sommer, Sally. "Tap Happy: Hines on *Tap*." *Dance Magazine*, December 1988.

"Sophisticated Ladies." *New York*, March 16, 1981.

Taitte, Lawson. "The Megadances Performances Kick Out the Jams." *The [Raleigh, NC] News and Observer*, January 11, 1998.

"TAP: Gregory Hines and Sammy Davis Jr. Co-Star in New Film." *Ebony*, February 1989.

"Tap Origins: A Brief History by Paul Corr." www.mcphu.edu/~corrp/tap/referenc.htm

Vespa, Mary. "Far from Running Scared, Dancer Gregory Hines Takes His First Great Leap as a Leading Man." *People*, August 11, 1986.

Wadler, Joyce. "Hines on *Tap*: When the Artist Steps into Movies." *Washington Post*, February 24, 1985.

Webb, Betty. "Hines Has Career in Comfortable Rhythm." *Tempe [Arizona] Daily News*, September 17, 1996.

INDEX

PICTURE CREDITS

GINA DE ANGELIS lives in Virginia and holds a bachelor's degree in theater and history and a master's degree in history. She is the author of several plays and screenplays as well as this biography, her eighth book for Chelsea House.

NATHAN IRVIN HUGGINS, one of America's leading scholars in the field of black studies, helped select the titles for the BLACK AMERICANS OF ACHIEVEMENT series, for which he also served as senior consulting editor. He was the W. E. B. DuBois Professor of History and Afro-American Studies at Harvard University and the director of the W. E. B. DuBois Institute for Afro-American Research at Harvard. He received his doctorate from Harvard in 1962 and returned there as professor in 1980 after teaching at Columbia University, the University of Massachusetts, Lake Forest College, and the California State University, Long Beach. He was the author of four books and dozens of articles, including *Black Odyssey: The Afro-American Ordeal in Slavery*, *The Harlem Renaissance*, and *Slave and Citizen: The Life of Frederick Douglass*, and was associated with the Children's Television Workshop, National Public Radio, the Boston Athenaeum, the Museum of Afro-American History, the Howard Thurman Educational Trust, and Upward Bound. Professor Huggins died in 1989, at the age of 62, in Cambridge, Massachusetts.